Talking
GOD
for no reason

MICHAEL JOSHUA

Talking With God for No Reason
Copyright © 2018 by Michael Joshua

Library of Congress Control Number: 2018957508
ISBN-13:   Paperback: 978-1-64398-356-1
            PDF: 978-1-64398-357-8
            ePub: 978-1-64398-358-5
            Kindle: 978-1-64398-359-2

Printed in the United States of America

LitFire LLC
1-800-511-9787
www.litfirepublishing.com
order@litfirepublishing.com

Contents

*B*EGINNING

Never wait for you life
to begin
Your life began
at birth
It will end
at death

Your life
almost always
will never be how you want
Awards
may go somewhere else
Your life remains
Kisses
may not be returned
Your life remains
Love
may not be taken
Your life remains

Love your life
Now
There is no time in the
after-life
to live
life

FEAR IN LOVE

My love
I get scared of the day
when you are no longer
My love
but
the love
of another
soul
sucking the kiss
of another kiss
feeling the form
of another shape

FEAR OF LOVE

I wish to reveal my love
only to myself
I love myself
as a person
should
love themself
I wonder if you will love
me
like
I love me
if
I reveal my love

CRAZY

Family thinks
you're crazy
Friends say
you're crazy
you begin to believe
but
you know you're not crazy
because
you know you're not crazy

ISOLATION

I just dont feel like
talking to anyone
right now
right here
I'm not sad
in fact
I'm enjoying
being by myself in this tiny cubicle
room listening to the singer sing his
song listening to the thoughts I forgot

ORDER

You are here
for GOD
GOD is not here
for you

OBVIOUS ANSWER

Would you rather have
ten million dollars
or
a regular dose of love and sex

7

ONSET OF A DEPRESSION

I have a sinking feeling falling deeper
within myself through a dark swirl
surrounding myself with twirling legs
flailing arms creating a whirlpool of
obscurity and failure

DISBELIEF OF LOVE

Tired of

flirting   talking
            complimenting   laughing
loving   suggesting
            hugging   caressing
touching   kissing
            fucking   listening
                  understanding

GOD, in STEPS

"Do you believe in God," I asked my
friend as he smoked his cigarettes
drank his drink as he thought drunk
        "No, I am God."
Astonished?
        Not at all, how could I
scream at this atheist when I myself
once didn't believe in God
        God reveals God in
slow steps   repeated thoughts
coincidences

If God was visible
        God would be fake
The idea of God
        is greater than
the image of God
        God
      surrounds us
      is in us
      but
    we are not God

MALCOLM X

Never be afraid
to be
wrong
controversial
hated
solitary
Everyone else might be wrong

HAPPINESS

Become
invisible
unaware
of
your life
your thoughts

Art Student

Maybe just maybe
this is all for waste I live for
something intangible— art—
and then again we come back to the
subject of
what is art
why do I live for art
why do I think for art
why do I think I could succeed
as an artist
then again

I come back to the idea that I believe
in something else
intangible—God—
there must be a reason
Art

MATERIALISTIC WOMEN

are
missing out on mad passionate naked
flesh
on
flesh
the   body
the   breath
the   love
of
a man

IN CANADA TO FIND AMERICA

Drunk observing
CANADA
as a pretty blonde drives listening to
song about love gone wrong
thinking of thoughts to think
only thinking
this must be wrong
This
This life
Why was I
drunk
poor
and driving
in CANADA
on a sunny Saturday
when I should be working to succeed
in becoming an American billionaire
instead I'm becoming
an American from the past
enjoying life enjoying freedom
in America
because
America offers freedom

Modern American
I am not
Modern Americans
are
money hungry
searching fame

LOVE OR IDEA OF LOVE

....

I get depressed in love I
never know if this is love or am I the
only one in love I dont understand
love or else I'm thinking too much
about love to actually feel love
I need to forget
consequences of love   I need to
forgive my love of faults   I need to
understand love is real love is free
Control love and like a caged tiger
love will escape

Hollow

There are times when I am exactly
like a lunatic bum fucking sick of life
sick of myself sick of God
I have no fucking control
of my words of my tears of my cry
I feel emotionless
a piece of jelly jiggling
with no end in sight aside from
madness

DAILY FEELINGS

Become immune to feelings
feelings are changing daily
never trust feelings
daily feelings are little fluttering bugs
wanting to bite and bleed as well as
bright glimmering sunshine
daily feelings
cause confusion
only trust overall beliefs about
yourself never daily feelings

UNGLAMOUROUS SANITY

If you want to save your sanity
Don't pursue fame
fame is picking up the shit of a shit
who doesn't even deserve the right to
be in the same room as yourself
but
due to poverty stricken circumstances
the shit will be picked up
without a sound
with a smile

LIFE'S MENTOR

My mentor is high above me
constantly
giving suggestions and
laughing
when
I dont listen
not mean laughing
but
friendly laughing

LIFE ADVICE

Follow
       your
              first
                     instinct

WHORES'S LIFE

I dont wish to fuck everyone
I'm tired of fucking everyone
I want to love and fuck
my soul-mate

ONE LIFE YOUR LIFE

Life is easy
if lived like the way you want to live
your life
Never live the life of someone else
Be yourself through life

Explain Experience

Never
let anyone else explain life to you
experience it yourself

MENTAL MARRIAGE

you I love
your love your smile your eyes
our style
your hair your care
as a woman as a girl as a mother
I will love you now
as we love
I will love you forever
when we separate

MAYBE, LOVE

Maybe it was me
Maybe it was you
Maybe it was in between
I thought it was hate
it might have been love
either way
it will remain
a maybe

LOVE, FOREVER

I love you
Why? Because
you were the one I was
always searching
but didn't know you existed
I love you
and
will always love you
because
you exist

REMINDER OF YOU

I saw you today sitting nakedly
unashamed in a bathing suit that
colored your tan southern frame
smiling cute dimples
I was seeing you by looking at
this southern princess
I love her
as much as
I loved you

IN THE GRAVE

In the end
I want to kiss
who I wanted
love who I wanted
touch who I wished

MODERN MARRIAGE OATH

I'm not going to
marry you
I'm just going to
die with you

BASIC

I love that
you love me as a child
and not
as a man
as a man I am not the man
as I am as a child

LIFE QUESTION?

Do you love yourself?

ANOTHER LIFESTYLE

I am positive I am a
negative lunatic raging dancing
drinking drugging sexing
positive
negative lunatic raging dancing
drinking drugging
women
We are having the time of our life
Why does anybody else care
We don't

SEXUALITY

If it wasn't for sex

you wouldn't be able
to read this

SONGWRITERS

Bruce Springsteen please ask
Michael Stipe Eddie Vedder
and other songwriters
to invoke the spirit of
Jim Morrison
Jimi Hendrix
Bob Marley
to only write songs which will make
Americans the people
The Beatles inspired
Kurt Cobain

Kurt Cobain I love you
but
you quit on yourself
and
you quit on me and the rest of
the stupid fucks that we were
leaving us no idea how to be us
Richard Ashcroft thank you
songwriters only write a song if you
can change the world

INSPIRATION

Become an inspiration of
Jack Kerouac
Jim Morrison James Dean
American Dreams
American Screams
to be Jesus to be free to be loved
by God
for being a person

CHILD TO PARENT

I didn't ask to be born
I could have been happy
never having been
since I'm born I'll live how I want
I will fuck suck
anything
that I want
why
I want to
You gave me life
I didn't ask to be born
My life is not your life
nor could it ever be
I want unique
You already have the life
you wanted to live that you want me
to live
I want uniqueness

TRUE LOVE

I need you
                    you don't need me
you need me
                    I don't need you
walk away if you wish

 WOMEN

Women make sure
      your men
      love you
      from the top of your toes to
      the bottom of your heart

No One Wants

No one wants
love
No one wants
truth
No one wants
excitement
to the point of working on these three
everyday

No one wants
power
No one wants
courage
No one wants
freedom
to the point of grinding the body to
the wheel and standing fast during the
storm
Who wants?

ORGASM

Coming to
the idea of heaven
inside your mind
through your body
here on earth

FIRST LOVE

Love
God
Yourself
Family
Strangers
Friends
Enemies
God

MEN,-TO WOMEN,-TO MEN

I am not a tag-along trophy for you
to feel good about yourself
about having me on your side
I am here because I want to be
not because I have to be
You are not the world
Treat me like the world
I'll give you the world

ALWAYS BE A CHILD

Adults think they cannot accomplish
what they know they
could have accomplished
as a child

FOREVER DREAMING

A dream never dies
only dreamers
dreams get transferred from
one mind to
another soul
another mind to
continue the dream

AMERICAN SONS

An American son chasing
American dreams American women
American times
smoking pot   drinking wine
pumping caffeine
to stay awake   stay dreaming
stay screaming
Parents
I apologize for being an American
son

DEATH

You will die
when God wants
you to die

BEING OLD WHILE YOUNG

I am aging myself
by suffering about nothing
by worrying about actions of others
my brothers my sisters my god
why was I worrying about other's?
worrying about me

LAST LOVE

This is in tribute to the one I loved
last
thank you for loving me for who I
was I had forgotten who I was
I had forgotten why I was alive
You showed me why

CONFUSED, LOVE

Confused love
constant
love is never simple
love is life
life is love
confusion
constant

IDEAS OF YOU

What is your idea of you
what is others idea of you
Are they the same idea
Do they think you
naughty or nice
heinous or bright beautiful or bland
Do you care if other ideas of you
match
your ideas of you

DISGUISED

How do I know God is working
Mother Theresa Dr. King Malcolm X
Lincoln Kennedy Lennon Roosevelt
Ghandi Kerouac Einstein Mozart
Pope John Paul
countless others
working through God
for God
for themselves

CREATION

Learn to stop hating yourself
for who you are not
Love yourself for what you are
If you weren't supposed to be you
God would have made you
someone else

A PERSON

Am I here
Am I alive

I feel invisible
invincible
unable to think differently
a lost child in a large lost world
insanely ecstatic to be lost in a lunatic
life

UNCONDITIONAL HEART

Perceive me in your eyes
love me with your heart
Hear me in your ears
listen to me with your heart
Remember me in your mind
think of me with your heart

ONE

The perfect world
No
countries flags religions
ethnicity colors categories
separation
All is one
different but same

My WIFE

my lover my best friend
my dream my hope my self
my psychologist my inspiration
my desire my twin my soul
my attention my focus
my pet my protection

CHANGING

Everything has changed
Everyone replaced
The past is all left back
People that you knew
Teachers that you met
come back
in a late night dream
I will soon be gone never to return
hopefully finding my place

GOD (pt. 3)

God are you listening
God what are you doing
is it all planned before
Can I see the blue-prints
God why me
does the world need me
God why these thoughts
God I trust
God I want to see you
I heard you
God
why poverty why sickness
why death why accidents
God will we ever meet face to face
God what's heaven
I know hell
earth
God I dont know
I wish I was born an orphan
I only like disappointing myself

RANDOM

Stop being frightened of death
It is even more frightening
not to live
Stop watching others
Create your own images
Physical Emotional Mental
Intellectual
Life is not a dress rehearsal

WAITING

Maybe---one day
You'll be waiting for me
Till then I'm still hoping
Meantime
          I'm asking questions
Should I hold on to past moments
In this waiting the past has become
my present
          I should move on
Time isn't waiting
          I've created wasted moments
I'll keep moving
          always remembering
How you kept me waiting

 MONOTONY

What I say today
has been already said
Please don't ask me to explain
I've explained it before

BEGGAR

We're not begging you
we're asking you
to give us a moment
to feel like we do
to live like we do
in shame
To live
without knowing if we exist

FRIENDSHIP

When friends are enemies
forgive
and
learn to forget

SHORTCOMINGS

Every man has
disappointments
Every man has to learn to accept
disappointments
By refusing acceptance
Man will lose focus of what was
accomplished

DEATH RESPECT

To dead heroes
who didn't know they'd change the
world
when they were breathing
life into others
meanwhile
losing grasp
of themselves

GENESIS

I want to be
natural   naked
I want to love you
for you
I want you to love me
for me
I play Adam You play Eve
No Apples
No Snakes
No God

RISKS

benefit of taking a risk
You'll meet the most interesting
person in the world
Yourself

DOUBTS REGRETS

In life
never regret anything
                    pursue everything you love
Failure is always admirable compared
to regrets
Fail everything—
                    Experience
            Regret everything—
                            Doubts
Experience yourself this life
Doubt absolutely nothing about
                    yourself
Your self---will never think doubts
—only thinks thoughts ideas
Thoughts Ideas—
            pursue
Regret in
            death
Live in
            life

BEING YOUNG IN AMERICA

The world is
large   enormous   unexplored
The people   The places
The experience of
being young   being American
being crazy
cannot be replaced monetarily
stop making money
explore America
millionaires die penniless

You
You I miss
on days like this
when you are
no where
near me

You
You I'm convinced
are me
Me
I'm you

You think
like me
You love
like me
If I was you
I would love me
No one else will love you
like you love you
except me

Dream # 4

I have gone to the other side of my
                            mind Although I
am slightly frightened
I am overly grateful
Life has a beginning
                before birth
Life has an ending
                before death
The twists   the turns
                connect and disjoin
at various points
coming full circle and separating
again in death
in after-life
Life never ends
        People never die
            Only get replaced
                by different masks   different
voices same observations
God in the form of
Jesus in the form of
Saints in the form of
Writers in the form of
Singers in the form of
Parents in the form of
Babies

REMEMBERING YOU
THROUGH A SONG

I heard the song
you said you could write
if you were a songwriter
as I sat in a hotel room alone
The sound of the station going
in and out
As the song ends
smile returns to my face
remembering you

INTERNAL EXTERNAL

It is not what happens to a man
but
what happens within a man

LET GO

To gain
understanding and freedom
lose sight of
the shore

FAR FROM LOVE

I am you
as you
are me
being away
being alone
from you
I
masturbate me because of you
as you masturbate me

*P*RIORITY THOUGHT

Would you rather
die like
Elvis
or
Jesus

POOR MAN'S BLUE'S

Love is not about the size of my
wallet it is about the size
of
me
inside
of
you

ABORTION

For each supposed Einstein
that is aborted
there are many more born that will
have to struggle more than necessary

If not used gratuitously
abortion should be a couple's choice

INTERTWINED MOODS

Repression
leads to depression
is connected to happiness
is correlated with loneliness

Egotistical Loneliness

He is in love with his libido
She is in love with her face
They make love by themselves
They are lonely
beyond reason
They are afraid to take the next step
They are afraid to let someone in
No other body can love them
like they love themselves

LIFE WITHOUT YOU

I'm going to
live   breathe   laugh   sing
    miss   cry   see   die
If you're with me if you're without
I'm still going to be
I might be torn apart
but
I'm going to
live   breathe   laugh   sing
    miss   cry   see   die

LONELY WOMAN SONG

Love is the reason for her questions
walking in anger
      searching for somebody
      searching for answers
screaming
      "I'd love you and I want you
      to make me feel alright"
Not easy watching
words flowing from mouth to mouth
Quiet
Listening in great surprise
Still no one by her side
Watching   Caring
Drinks alone in a hollow noise
Crowds gathering around her side
Yelling   Kicking
     Waiting   Wanting
to scream

     "I'd love you and I want
you   to take me away to a
forgotten place"

83

SEARCHING FOR YOURSELF

It might make me feel sick
It might make me feel clean
I know I'm uncertain I might be
insane
My body is aching and so is my brain
I'm not sure if I'm living
know I'm not dead
I wanted to find me
Would I be the same

CONNECT

Discuss   Discussing
to remember why we were born
Learn   Learning
to forget why we should die
Speak   Speaking
to get your point out from within
Listen   Listening
to give someone else a chance
See   Seeing
to view the beauty around
Love   Loving
to be unselfish to others

Cry   Crying
to wait for a better tomorrow
Sleep   Sleeping
to keep the dream alive

LOST SOUL

I hate God
I don't understand God
I wish for love
I wish for happiness
I wish for perfection
wish for fortunes
I wish for everything
I find emptiness
in my friends in my love
in my self

DREAM LIVING

When you start to live
what you are dreaming
is when you believe
you are living

Someday soon

We will reach the sun
someday soon
fast
while we are young

Touch the hands
which feed from high
bless our souls
keep us warm

CONFUSED YOUTH

I am fake
I am invisible
I am dying
I am nothing I wish to be

I am unwanted
I am unloved
I am exactly as I dont want to be

I am un-understandable

GROUPED INDIVIDUALITY

Individuality is dying
everyone is a group a section a
column a separation
Individuals are dead
or
dying

WHO ARE YOU WHO AM I

Where to belong
do you belong
black   white   yellow   brown
gay   bi   lesbian   straight
Buddhist   Sikh   Atheist   Catholic
Baptist   Protestant   Scientist
tall   fat   ugly   beautiful   short
deformed

why belong

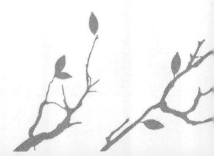

QUOTATION FROM GAYFRIENDS

They don't think it strange
they're both quite sexual
She only wants her
He only wants him
Nothing is strange from their own
point of view

The people just stare
wonder what is wrong
when a boy is doing
what a girl should have done
These two don't care
nothing is wrong
They have their own way
of living their own days
If the people are staring
they say let them keep staring

they say —this is my life
I am not hurting their life
they don't need to care
they don't need to understand
this is the way we live our life
we don't wonder how you life your
life
please don't stare
but
we don't care
it does not bother us
it only bothers you
she says—I wish I was him
he says—I wish I was her
she says —I am in love with
the girl he should love
he is in love with the boy I should
love

Bliss

Complete happiness
Naked
flesh on flesh
soft touches
legs wrapped around
back
pulsating to music
words meaning truth
ears believing
love you
Feeling heaven
Feeling complete
Sexual inspiration
understanding silence
meaningful sculptured art
unafraid to be naked
physically emotionally spiritually
movie scene which the mind
photographed for a lifetime never to
be duplicated

MILLION MILES AN HOUR

Thinking of running away thinking of
dropping out wanting to be
somewhere else wanting to be
someone else
been through everything been through
the unexplained hoping for someone's
help waiting for someone to let go
don't know what I want anymore
I heard the singer scream
I don't know what I want anymore
I heard within myself

MAYBE DEAD MAYBE ALIVE

Maybe there is some way not to die
We keep running in the sky with
questions in our head as we finally
meet our God
What are the questions you will ask

Ingram Content Group UK Ltd.
Milton Keynes UK
UKHW042019090323
418309UK00001B/114